BIG BOOK OF SMASH HITS 2004-05

Published by
Music Sales Limited
8/9 Frith Street, London W1D 3JB, England

Exclusive Distributors:
Music Sales Limited
Distribution Centre, Newmarket Road,
Bury St. Edmunds, Suffolk IP33 3YB, England.
Music Sales Pty Limited
120 Rothschild Avenue, Rosebery, NSW 2018, Australia.

Order No. AM91732
ISBN 0-7119-3848-2
This book © Copyright 2004 by Wise Publications

Compiled by Nick Crispin.
Arranged by Derek Jones & Jack Long.
Music processed by Paul Ewers Music Design.
Cover illustration courtesy Paul Clarke.
Printed and bound in Malta by Interprint Ltd.

Your Guarantee of Quality
As publishers, we strive to produce every book to the highest commercial
standards. Throughout, the printing and binding have been planned to ensure a
sturdy, attractive publication which should give years of enjoyment. If your copy
fails to meet our high standards, please inform us and we will gladly replace it.

GW00500348

This publication is not authorised for sale in the
United States of America and/or Canada.

WISE PUBLICATIONS
part of The Music Sales Group

London/New York/Sydney/Paris/Copenhagen/Berlin/Madrid/Tokyo

ALL THESE THINGS THAT I'VE DONE

Words & Music by Brandon Flowers, Dave Keuning, Mark Stoermer & Ronnie Vannucci

hold on, ___ if you can ___ hold on, ___ hold on. ___

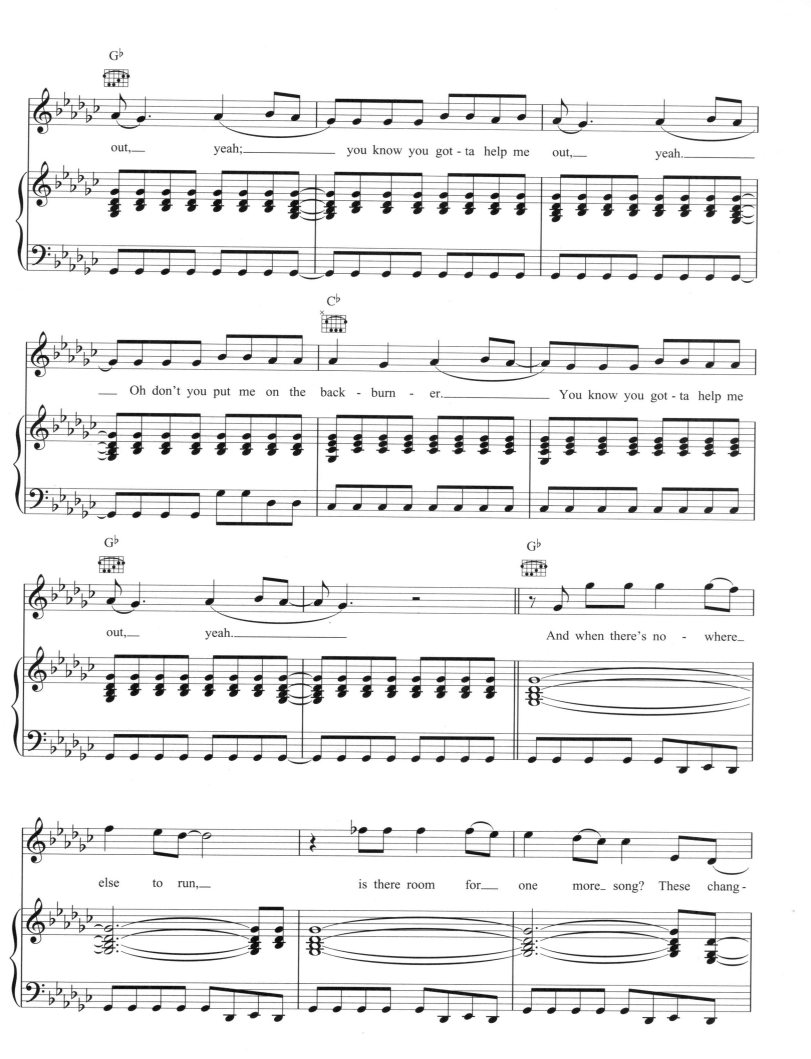

5

-es   ain't   chang - ing me: the cold heart-ed boy I

used   to be.   Yeah,   you know you got - ta help me

out,   yeah.   Oh don't you put me on the back - burn - er.

   You know you got - ta help me out,   yeah.   You're gon - na bring your-self

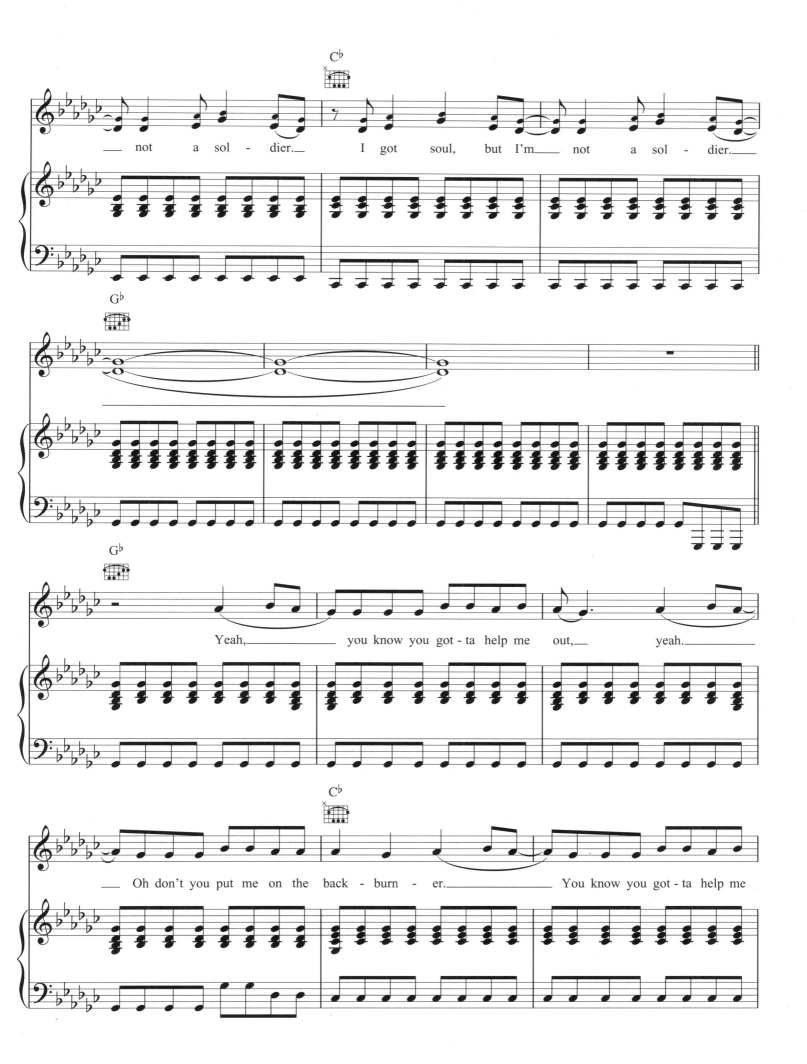

not a sol - dier. I got soul, but I'm not a sol - dier.

Yeah, you know you got - ta help me out, yeah.

Oh don't you put me on the back - burn - er. You know you got - ta help me

out,___ yeah.___ You're gon-na bring your-self___ down. Yeah,___

___ you're gon-na bring your-self___ down, yeah.___ Oh don't you put me on the

back - burn - er.___ You're gon-na bring your-self___ down. Yeah,___

___ you're gon-na bring your-self down. Ov - er and in,___

last_____ call for sin._____ While ev-'ry-one's

lost, the bat-tle is won with all these things that I've___ done;___

_____ all these

things that I've___ done.___

If you can___ hold___ on.___

If you can___ hold   on.___

BUTTERFLIES AND HURRICANES

Words & Music by Matthew Bellamy, Chris Wolstenholme & Dominic Howard

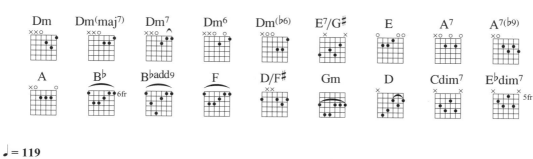

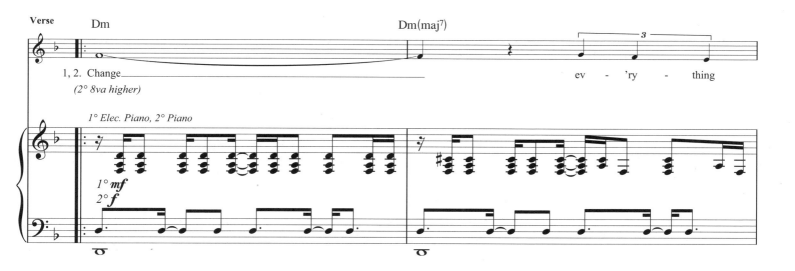

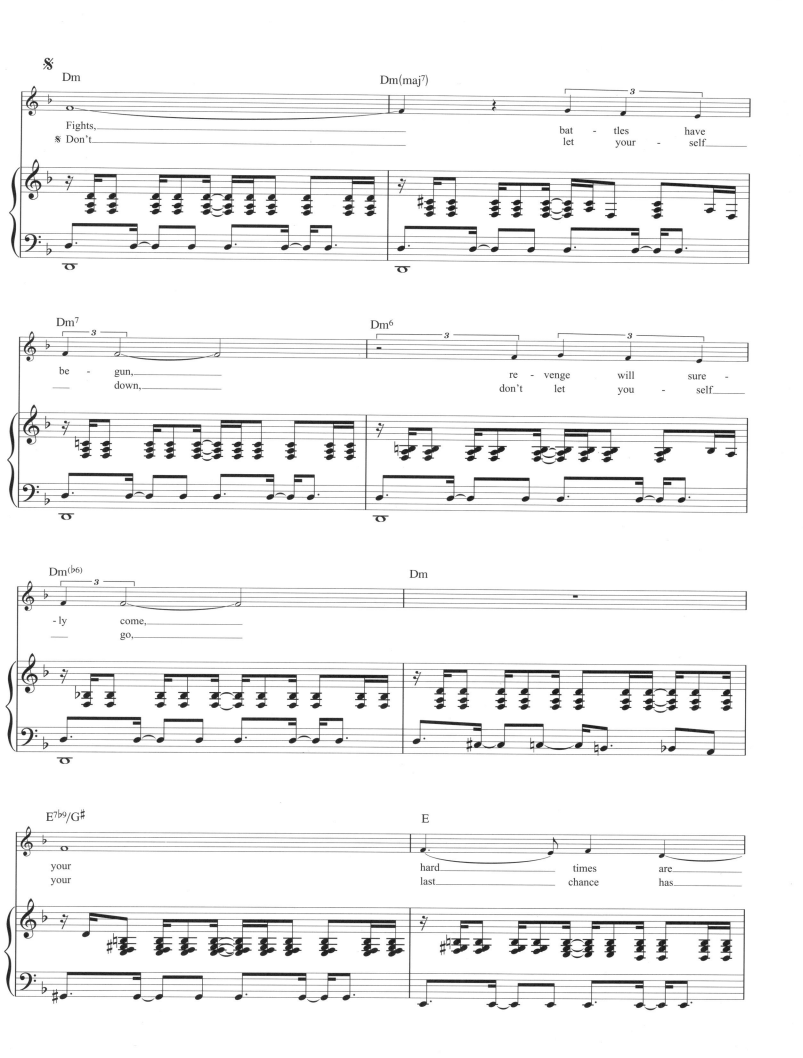

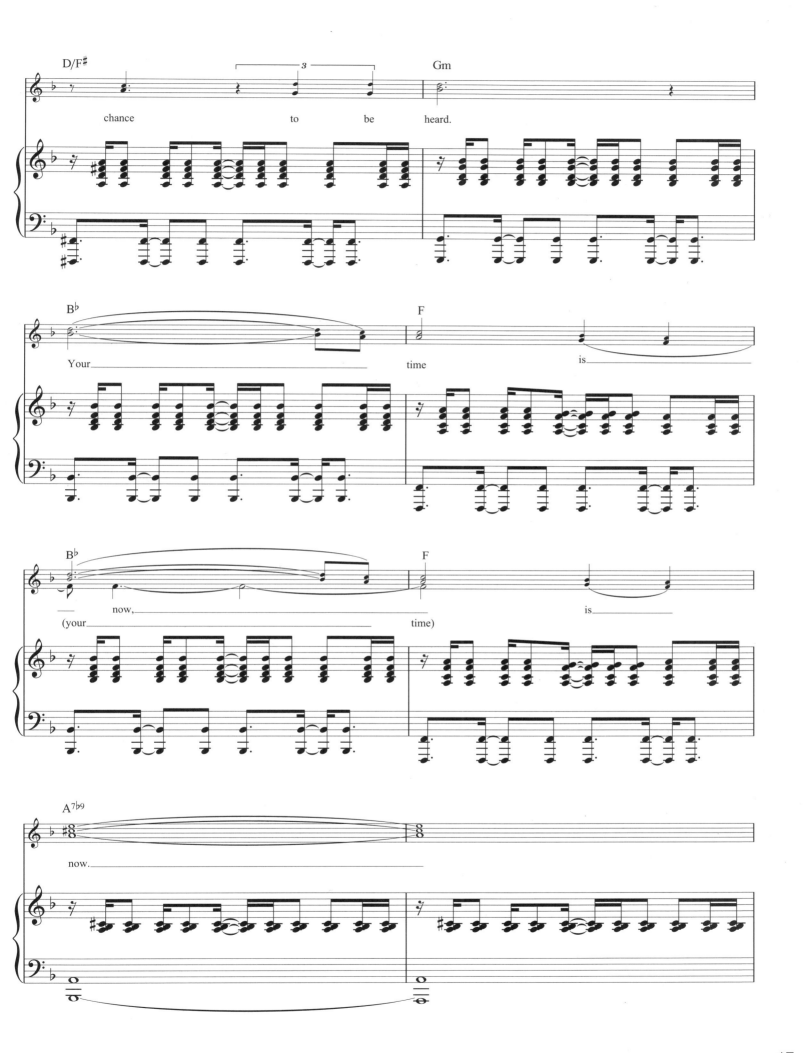

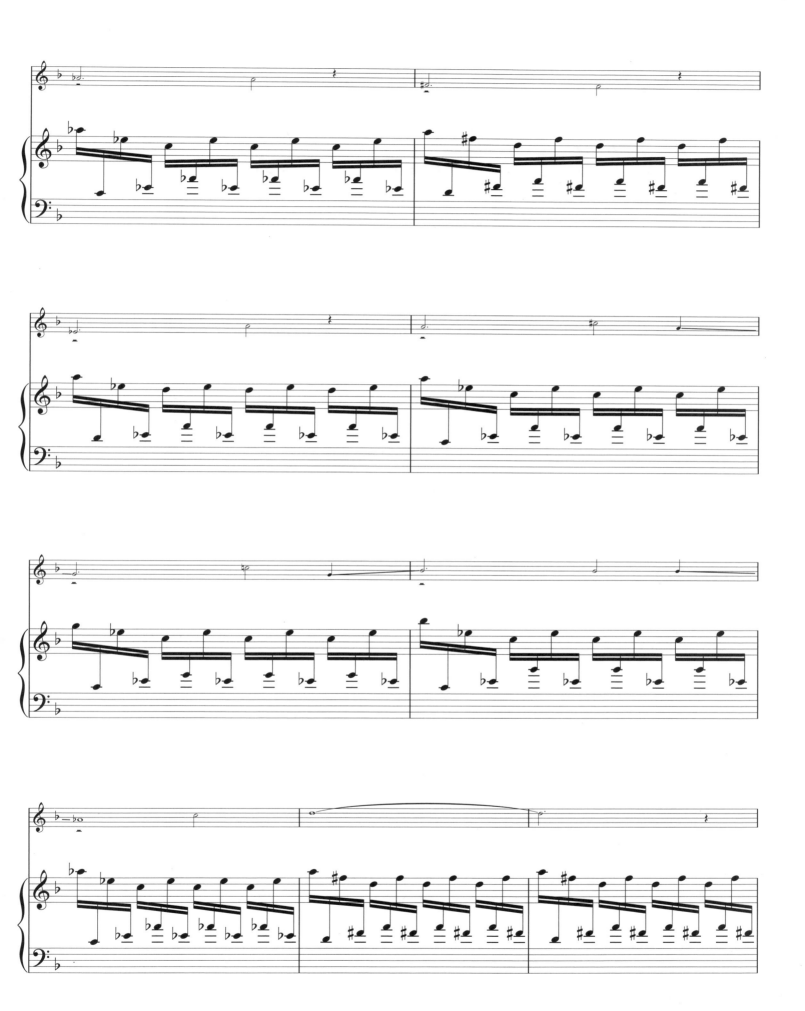

BEDSHAPED

Words & Music by Tim Rice-Oxley, Tom Chaplin, Richard Hughes & James Sanger

Lyrics:

1. Ma-ny's the time__ I ran__ with you down__ the rain -
(2.) know you think__ I'm hold - ing you down__ and I've

To Coda ⊕

2. I know,

Vocoder

25

CAUGHT IN A MOMENT

Words & Music by Karen Poole, Keisha Buchanan, Johnny Lipsey,
Mutya Buena, Heidi Range & Marius De Vries

make or break, boy, here and now.
step by step, boy, here and now.
We're caught in a

mo - ment, and I won't let it go.
I am

fall - ing deep and los - ing my con - trol,
in - volved in a

feel - ing like the blink of an eye.
And the

no_____ turn - ing___ back.   And now I'm shed-ding all my fears____   I know,___

I know_____ we're caught in a

COME AS YOU ARE

Words & Music by Beverley Knight & Guy Chambers

in - side a cool dark space.___ Ah, ah, ah.___
don't want to make no mess.___ No, no, no.___

E   B   F#

Yeah, sum - mer's be - gun,___ this is where one___ needs to be two.___
Yeah, sum - mer's be - gun,___ we could have fun___ play - ing for kicks.

G#   E   B

___ Yeah, I know I'm bold,___ but ba - by I'm sold___
___ Yeah, ha - bits to feed___ and ba - by I need_

F#   G#   E

___ on me___ with you.___ }   Come as you are,___ you_
___ to get___ my fix.___ }

'bout. Hey, hey._____ *Instrumental/Vocal ad lib.*

D.S. al Coda

Come as you are,

Coda

Instrumental/Vocal ad lib.

Repeat ad lib.

DON'T LEAVE HOME

Words & Music by Dido Armstrong & Rollo Armstrong

1. Like a ghost, don't need a key. Your best friend I've come to be.

when it's just___ you and lit - tle me.

Ev - 'ry - thing is clear___ and ev - 'ry - thing is new,

so you won't___ be leav - ing will___ you.

D.S. al Coda

And if you're

Coda

home.

'Cause I___ will___ be your___

cont. sim.

DRY YOUR EYES

Words & Music by Mike Skinner

1. In one single moment your whole life can turn 'round. I stand there for a minute staring straight into the ground,
(Verses 2 & 3 see block lyrics)

looking to the left slightly then looking back down. World feels like it's caved in, proper sorry frown.

Please let me show you where we could only just be for us. I can change and I can grow or we could adjust.

The wicked thing about us is we always have trust, we can even have an open relationship if you must.

I look at her, she stares almost straight back at me, but her eyes glaze over like she's looking straight through me

Then her eyes must have closed for what seems an eternity. When they open up she's looking down at her feet.

Dry your eyes__ mate, I know it's hard to take__ but her__ mind has__ been made__ up. There's plen - ty__ more fish__ in the sea.

Dry your eyes__ mate, I know you want to make__ her see__ how much__ this pain__ hurts. But you've got to walk__ a - way now. It's ov - er.__

To Coda

I know— you want to make her see how much this pain hurts.

But you've got to walk— a - way now.

Verse 2:

So then I moved my hand up from down by my side
Shaking, my life was crashing before my eyes
Turned the palm of my hand up to face the skies
Touched the bottom of her chin and let out a sigh
'Cause I can't imagine my life without you and me
There's things I can't imagine doing and things I can't imagine seeing
It weren't supposed to be easy surely?
Please, please I'm begging, please
She brings her hands up towards where my hands rested
She wraps her fingers 'round mine with the softness she's blessed with
She peels away my fingers, looks at me and then gestures
By pushing my hand away to my chest from hers.

Verse 3:

Trying to pull her close out of bare desperation
Put my arms around her, trying to change what she's saying
Pull my head level with hers so she might engage in
Look into her eyes to make her listen again.
I'm not gonna fuckin', just fuckin' leave it all now
'Cause you said it would be forever and that was your vow
And you're gonna let our thing simply crash and fall down
You're well out of order now, this is well out of town.
She pulls away my arms are tightly clamped around her waist
Gently pushes me back as she looks at me straight
Turns around so she's now got her back to my face
Takes one step forward, looks back and then walks away.

EVERYTIME

Words & Music by Britney Spears & Annette Stamatelatos

Please for- give me._____ And my weak - ness caused_ you pain_

and this song's_ my sor - ry._____

rit.

D.S. al Coda

Coda

51

F**K IT
(I DON'T WANT YOU BACK)

Words & Music by Eamon Doyle, Kirk Robinson & Mark Passy

GOLDEN TOUCH

Words & Music by Johnny Borrell

1. I know a girl____ with the gold-en touch.____
2. That kind of girl,____ yes, she's nev-er a - lone.____

She's got e - nough, she's got____ too much.____
You leave a thou-sand mes-sa-ges on her phone.____

But then all

C#m   B   A

they know   is how to put you down.

F#m   G#m   C#m   B

When you're there,   they're your friend;   but

A   F#m   G#m   C#m

then, when you're not a - round,   they say "Oh,   she's

well.

I saw my girl____ with the gold - en touch

60

GRAVITY

Words & Music by Guy Berryman, Chris Martin, Jon Buckland & Will Champion

don't   look_____ down.   And then I__
won't   look_____ down.   And then I__

__ looked up at the sun___ and I could see____   oh the way__
__ looked up at the sun___ and I could see____   oh the way__

__ that gra - vi - ty turns___ for you and me.____   And then I__
__ that gra - vi - ty turns___ on you and me.____   And then I__

__ looked up at the sky___ and saw the sun,____   and the way__
__ looked up at the sun___ and saw the sky,____   and the way__

that gra-vi-ty pulls on ev-'ry one, on ev-'ry one.

that gra-vi-ty pulls on you and I,

on you and I.

OBVIOUSLY

Words & Music by James Bourne, Thomas Fletcher & Danny Jones

out of this world,___ be - lieve me._____

2. She's got a boy - friend___ he drives her round the___ bend;___
3. Got to es - cape now,___ get on a plane now___

'cause he's twen - ty three,___ he's
off to L. A.,___ and

in the Ma - rines,___ he'd kill me._____
that's where I'll stay___ for two years._____

good e - nough for her,____ no, no.____ I
good e - nough for her,____ no, no.____ I

1.

nev - er will be good e - nough for her.____
nev - er will be

2.

good e - nough for her._____

N.C.

She's out of my hands,_____ and I nev - er know where I

MY HAPPY ENDING

Words & Music by Avril Lavigne & Butch Walker

OUR LIVES

Words & Music by Aaron Kamin & Alex Band

Yeah,___ is it not worth the___ risk?___

No? Yeah!___

'Cause these are the days___ worth liv - ing,___ these are the years___

___ we're giv - en;___ and these are the mo - ments, these are the times.___

RADIO

Words & Music by Robbie Williams & Stephen Duffy

shout out some - thing. Lis - ten to the ra - di - o____ and

you will hear the songs____ you know.____ Make it ef - fer - ves-

- cent here____ and you might have a job____ my dear.____

My dear.____

1.
N.C.

2. I'm

I can feel__ it. Mov - ing out__ of time__ you'll hear__ it.

Fall - ing in_____ the way_____ you fear____ it.

Jump - ing, thump - ing, shout out some - thing.

Lis - ten to the ra - di - o_____ then you will hear the songs__

you know. Make it ef - fer - ves - cent here___ and

you might have a job___ my dear.___ Lis - ten to the ra -

- di - o.___ Lis - ten to the ra - di - o.___

Lis - ten to the ra - di - o.___

N.C.

Drums

THUNDERBIRDS

Words & Music by Barry Gray, Charles Simpson,
Matthew Sargeant, James Bourne & Thomas Fletcher

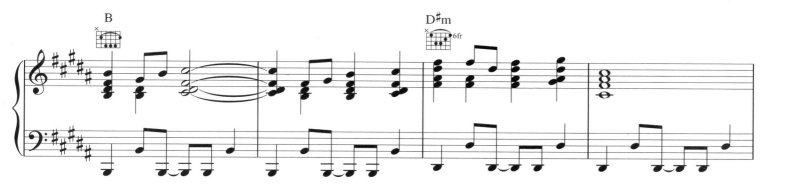

now   the   boys are back_ in town,___   no   strings to hold_ them

down,_____   down._____

Don't   be____ mad,__ please   stop   the____ hat - ing

just   be____ glad___ that   they'll   be____ wait - ing.

Thun - der - birds___ are go.___

Thun - der - birds___ are go.___

Thun - der - birds___ are, Thun - der -

birds___ are, Thun - der - birds___ are go.

SHE WILL BE LOVED

Words & Music by Adam Levine, James Valentine,
Jesse Carmichael, Mickey Madden & Ryan Dusick

I know that good-bye means no-thing at all, comes back and begs me, catch her ev-'ry time she falls. Yeah.

Tap on my win-dow, knock on my door I want to make you feel beau - ti - ful.

D.S. al Coda

SICK AND TIRED

Words & Music by Glen Ballard, Dallas Austin & Anastacia Newkirk

My love is on the line,

my love is on the line My love is on the line, my love is on the line.

My love is on the line. My love.

114

YOU HAD ME

Words & Music by Francis White, Joss Stone, Betty Wright & W. Stoker

WHATEVER HAPPENED TO COREY HAIM?

Words by Conor Deasy
Music by Conor Deasy, Kevin Horan, Pádraic McMahon, Daniel Ryan & Ben Carrigan